HOLT
3
FRENCH

Allez, viens!®

Alternative Assessment Guide

HOLT, RINEHART AND WINSTON

A Harcourt Classroom Education Company

Austin • New York • Orlando • Atlanta • San Francisco • Boston • Dallas • Toronto • London

Contributing Writer

Portfolio Activities   Catharine Dallas Purdy
                            Austin, TX

Copyright © by Holt, Rinehart and Winston

All rights reserved. No part of this publication may be reproduced or transmitted in any form or by any means, electronic or mechanical, including photocopy, recording, or any information storage and retrieval system, without permission in writing from the publisher.

Teachers using ALLEZ, VIENS! may photocopy Scoring Rubrics in complete pages in sufficient quantities for classroom use only and not for resale.

Cover Photo Credits
Group of students: Marty Granger/HRW Photo; paint brushes: Image Copyright © 2003 Photodisc, Inc.; CD: Digital imagery® © 2003 Photodisc, Inc.

ALLEZ, VIENS! is a trademark licensed to Holt, Rinehart and Winston, registered in the United States of America and/or other jurisdictions.

Printed in the United States of America

ISBN 0-03-065569-2

3   4   5   6   7   066   05   04   03

Contents

Copyright © by Holt, Rinehart and Winston. All rights reserved.

To the Teacher

Individual students have individual needs and ways of learning, and progress at different rates in the development of their oral and written skills. The *Alternative Assessment Guide* is designed to accommodate those differences, and to offer opportunities for all students to be evaluated in the most favorable light possible and under circumstances that enable them to succeed. The *Alternative Assessment Guide* contains information and suggestions for assessing student progress in two ways that go beyond the standard quizzes and tests: portfolio assessment and performance assessment. Each section of the guide contains some general information and specific, chapter-related suggestions for incorporating each type of assessment into your instructional plan.

Portfolio Assessment

Student portfolios are of great benefit to foreign language students and teachers alike because they provide documentation of a student's efforts, progress, and achievements over a given period of time. In addition, students can receive both positive feedback and constructive criticism by sharing their portfolios with teachers, family, and peers. The opportunity for self-reflection provided by using a portfolio encourages students to participate in their learning in a positive way, thus fostering pride, ownership, and self-esteem.

This guide includes a variety of materials that will help you implement and assess student portfolios. The written and oral activity evaluation forms, student and teacher checklists, peer editing rubric, and portfolio evaluation sheets included here are designed for use with student portfolios, or for independent use as part of any assessment program.

Determining a Purpose

The first step in implementing the portfolios in your classroom is to determine the purpose for which they will be used. You can use portfolios to assess individual students' growth and progress, to make students active in the assessment process, to provide evidence and documentation of students' work for more effective communication with parents, or to evaluate an instructional program or curriculum. Both the contents of the portfolio and the manner in which it is to be evaluated will depend directly on the purpose(s) the portfolio is to serve. Before including any work in their portfolios, students should understand the purpose of the portfolio and the criteria by which their work will be evaluated.

Setting up the Portfolios

While portfolios can be used to meet a variety of objectives, they are especially useful tools for assessing written and oral work. Written items can be in a variety of formats including lists, posters, personal correspondence, poems, stories, articles, and essays, depending on the level and needs of the students. Oral items, such as conversations, interviews, commercials, and skits, may be recorded on audio- or videocassette for incorporation into the portfolio. Whatever the format, both written and oral work can include evidence of the developmental process, such as notes from brainstorming, outlines, early drafts, or scripts, as well as the finished product.

Each student can be responsible for keeping the materials selected for his or her portfolio. Encourage students to personalize the presentation of their portfolios and to keep in mind that their portfolios may include audiocassettes, videocassettes, or diskettes, as well as papers.

Selecting Materials for the Portfolio

There are several ways you and your students can select materials to include in portfolios. The portfolio should not be seen as a repository for all student work. Work to be included should be selected on the basis of the portfolio's purpose and evaluation criteria to be used.

Copyright © by Holt, Rinehart and Winston. All rights reserved.

Student Selection   Many teachers prefer to let students choose samples of their best work to include in their portfolios. Early in the year, you may tell students how many written and oral items to include in their portfolios (for example, one written item and one oral item per chapter) and allow students the freedom to choose those pieces that they feel best represent their ability in the language. In this case, the written and oral portfolio items suggested in this guide would be treated as any other writing or speaking activities, and students would have the option to include these in their portfolios. This option empowers students by allowing them to decide what to include in their portfolios. The feeling of ownership of the portfolio is likely to increase as the students' involvement at the decision-making level increases.

Teacher-Directed Selection   Some teachers prefer to maintain portfolios that contain students' responses to specific prompts or activities. The oral and written portfolio items suggested in this guide, or other writing or speaking activities of your choice, could be assigned specifically for inclusion in the portfolio. This type of portfolio allows you to focus attention on specific functions, vocabulary items, and grammar points.

Collaborative Selection   A third option is some combination of the two approaches described above. You can assign specific activities from which students may choose a pre-determined number of assignments to include in their portfolios, or you can assign some specific activities and allow the students to choose others on their own. The collaborative approach allows you to focus on specific objectives, while at the same time giving students the opportunity to showcase what they feel is their best work.

As the classroom teacher, you are in the best position to decide what type of portfolio is most beneficial for your program and students. The most important step is to decide what objectives and outcomes the portfolio should assess, and then assign or help students select items that will best reflect those objectives and outcomes.

Chapter-Specific Portfolio Suggestions

Specific portfolio suggestions, one written and one oral, are provided for each chapter. These suggestions are based on existing *Pupil's Edition* activities that have been expanded to incorporate most of the functions and the vocabulary for each chapter. These materials may be included in the students' portfolios or used as guidelines for the inclusion of other materials.

Using the Portfolio Checklists

The checklists on pages 12 and 13 will help you and your students keep their portfolios organized. The *Student's Portfolio Checklist* is designed to help students track the items they include. The *Teacher's Portfolio Checklist* is a list of the items you expect students to include. If you choose to allow students to select materials for their portfolios, your checklist will be very general, specifying only the types of items and the dates on which each item should be included. Your checklist will be more specific if you are assigning specific portfolio activities, as it should indicate the particular activities you have assigned and the dates on which they are to be included.

Peer Editing

Peer editing provides students an opportunity to help each other develop writing skills. It also promotes an atmosphere of responsibility and teamwork through the writing process. We have included a *Peer Editing Rubric* to encourage peer editing in the classroom, and to aid students in this part of the evaluation process. Using the rubric, students can exchange compositions (usually a first draft), and edit each other's work according to a clearly designed step-by-step process. The rubric is divided into three parts. Part I helps students examine the overall content of the written assignment using specific question prompts concerning vocabulary, organization, detail, and description. Part II helps students examine grammar and mechanics. In this part, you can tailor the goal of the assignment by outlining for the students the specific functions and grammar on which their editing should focus. For example, in Chapter 3, you might choose to focus on the subjunctive, or, in Chapter 4, you might choose functions for asking for and giving opinions. Use the space labeled "Target Functions and Grammar" in

Copyright © by Holt, Rinehart and Winston. All rights reserved.

Part 1 of the *Peer Editing Rubric* for this purpose. Part III asks students to discuss the first two parts of the rubric in an effort to have them evaluate each other's work critically. Even though the rubric is organized in a step-by-step manner, your help in addressing students' questions will further increase the effectiveness of the peer editing process. The *Peer Editing Rubric* can be used with any written assignment.

Documenting Group Work

Very often a group-work project cannot be included in an individual's portfolio because of its size or the difficulties involved in making copies for each group member (posters, bulletin boards, videos, and so on). Other group or pair activities, such as conversations or skits, cannot be included in the portfolio unless they are recorded. To help students document such activities in their portfolios, you may want to use the *Documentation of Group Work* form on page 11.

Evaluating the Total Portfolio

Exactly how and how often you evaluate your students' portfolios will depend on the stated purpose. Ideally, students' portfolios should be evaluated at regular intervals over the course of the academic year. You should establish the length of the assessment period in advance—six weeks, a quarter, a semester, and so on. The *Portfolio Self-Evaluation and Portfolio Evaluation* forms on pages 14–15 are designed to aid you and your students in assessing the portfolio at the end of each assessment period. In order to ensure that portfolios are progressing successfully, you might want to meet individually with each student throughout each assessment period. In addition, individual conferences with students should be scheduled at the end of each evaluation period to discuss their portfolios and compare your assessment with their own.

Performance Assessment

Performance assessment provides an alternative to traditional testing methods by using authentic situations as contexts for performing communicative, competency-based tasks. For every chapter of the *Pupil's Edition,* this guide provides performance assessment suggestions to go with each **étape** of the chapter and one suggestion for global performance assessment that involves vocabulary and functions from the entire chapter. These suggestions give students the opportunity to demonstrate acquired language proficiency and cultural competence in interviews, conversations, dialogues, or skits that can be performed for the entire class, or recorded or videotaped for evaluation at a later time. Performance assessment recordings can be included in student portfolios or used independently, according to your needs for oral evaluation.

Using CD-ROM for Assessment

The *Allez, viens! Interactive CD-ROM Tutor* provides a unique tool for evaluating students' language proficiency and for incorporating technology in the classroom. CD-ROM technology appeals to a variety of students learning styles and offers you an efficient means by which to gauge student progress. This guide provides instructions for written activities, such as lists, letters, e-mail, journal entries, and advertisements. Oral activities include conversations, interviews, and dialogues. Writing and recording features also enable you to create your own activities and to evaluate student work according to your particular needs. Student work can be saved to a disk and included in students' portfolios.

Copyright © by Holt, Rinehart and Winston. All rights reserved.

Rubrics and Evaluation Guidelines

Oral Rubric A

Use the following criteria to evaluate recorded assignments. For assignments where comprehension is difficult to evaluate, you might want to give students full credit for comprehension or weigh other categories more heavily.

	4	**3**	**2**	**1**
Content	**Complete**	**Generally complete**	**Somewhat complete**	**Incomplete**
	Speaker consistently uses the appropriate functions and vocabulary necessary to communicate.	Speaker usually uses the appropriate functions and vocabulary necessary to communicate.	Speaker sometimes uses the appropriate functions and vocabulary necessary to communicate.	Speaker uses few of the appropriate functions and vocabulary necessary to communicate.
Comprehension	**Total comprehension**	**General comprehension**	**Moderate comprehension**	**Little comprehension**
	Speaker understands all of what is said to him or her.	Speaker understands most of what is said to him or her.	Speaker understands some of what is said to him or her.	Speaker understands little of what is said to him or her.
Comprehensibility	**Comprehensible**	**Usually comprehensible**	**Sometimes comprehensible**	**Seldom comprehensible**
	Listener understands all of what the speaker is trying to communicate.	Listener understands most of what the speaker is trying to communicate.	Listener understands less than half of what the speaker is trying to communicate.	Listener understands little of what the speaker is trying to communicate.
Accuracy	**Accurate**	**Usually accurate**	**Sometimes accurate**	**Seldom accurate**
	Speaker uses language correctly including grammar, spelling, word order, and punctuation.	Speaker usually uses language correctly including grammar, spelling, word order, and punctuation.	Speaker has some problems with language usage.	Speaker makes many errors in language usage.
Fluency	**Fluent**	**Moderately fluent**	**Somewhat fluent**	**Not fluent**
	Speaker speaks clearly without hesitation. Pronunciation and intonation sound natural.	Speaker has few problems with hesitation, pronunciation, and/or intonation.	Speaker has some problems with hesitation, pronunciation, and/or intonation.	Speaker hesitates frequently and struggles with pronunciation and intonation.

French 3 Allez, viens!

Copyright © by Holt, Rinehart and Winston. All rights reserved.

Oral Rubric B

Assignment _____

Targeted function(s) _____

_____

Targeted vocabulary _____

Targeted grammar _____

Content	You used the functions and vocabulary necessary to communicate.	(Excellent)	4	3	2	1	(Poor)
Comprehension	You understood what was said to you and responded appropriately.	(Excellent)	4	3	2	1	(Poor)
Comprehensibility	The listener was able to understand what you were trying to communicate.	(Excellent)	4	3	2	1	(Poor)
Accuracy	You used language correctly including grammar, spelling, word order, and punctuation.	(Excellent)	4	3	2	1	(Poor)
Fluency	You spoke clearly and without hesitation. Your pronunciation and intonation sounded natural.	(Excellent)	4	3	2	1	(Poor)

Total Score _____

Comments _____

_____

_____

Copyright © by Holt, Rinehart and Winston. All rights reserved.

Oral Progress Report

OVERALL IMPRESSION

☐ Excellent   ☐ Good   ☐ Satisfactory   ☐ Unsatisfactory

Some particularly good aspects of this item are _____

_____

_____

_____

_____

Some areas that could be improved are _____

_____

_____

_____

_____

To improve your speaking, I recommend _____

_____

_____

_____

_____

Additional Comments _____

_____

_____

_____

_____

_____

Copyright © by Holt, Rinehart and Winston. All rights reserved.

Written Rubric A

Use the following criteria to evaluate written assignments.

	4	**3**	**2**	**1**
Content	**Complete**	**Generally complete**	**Somewhat complete**	**Incomplete**
	Writer uses the appropriate functions and vocabulary for the topic.	Writer usually uses the appropriate functions and vocabulary for the topic.	Writer uses few of the appropriate functions and vocabulary for the topic.	Writer uses none of the appropriate functions and vocabulary for the topic.
Comprehensibility	**Comprehensible**	**Usually comprehensible**	**Sometimes comprehensible**	**Seldom comprehensible**
	Reader can always understand all of what the writer is trying to communicate.	Reader can understand most of what the writer is trying to communicate.	Reader can understand less than half of what the writer is trying to communicate.	Reader can understand little of what the writer is trying to communicate.
Accuracy	**Accurate**	**Usually accurate**	**Sometimes accurate**	**Seldom accurate**
	Writer uses grammar, spelling, word order, and punctuation correctly.	Writer usually uses grammar, spelling, word order, and punctuation correctly.	Writer has some problems with language usage.	Writer makes a significant number of errors in language usage.
Organization	**Well-organized**	**Generally well-organized**	**Somewhat organized**	**Poorly organized**
	Presentation is logical and effective.	Presentation is generally logical and effective with a few minor problems.	Presentation is somewhat illogical and confusing in places.	Presentation lacks logical order and organization.
Effort	**Excellent effort**	**Good effort**	**Moderate effort**	**Minimal effort**
	Writer exceeds the requirements of the assignment and has put care and effort into the process.	Writer fulfills all of the requirements of the assignment.	Writer fulfills some of the requirements of the assignment.	Writer fulfills few of the requirements of the assignment.

Copyright © by Holt, Rinehart and Winston. All rights reserved.

Written Rubric B

Assignment _____

Targeted function(s) _____

_____

Targeted vocabulary _____

Targeted grammar _____

Content	You used the functions and vocabulary necessary to communicate.	(Excellent)	4	3	2	1	(Poor)	
Comprehensibility	The reader was able to understand what you were trying to communicate.	(Excellent)	4	3	2	1	(Poor)	
Accuracy	You used grammar, vocabulary, and functions accurately.	(Excellent)	4	3	2	1	(Poor)	
Organization	Your presentation was logical and effective.	(Excellent)	4	3	2	1	(Poor)	
Effort	You put a lot of thought and effort into this assignment.	(Excellent)	4	3	2	1	(Poor)	

Total Score _____

Comments _____

_____

_____

_____

Copyright © by Holt, Rinehart and Winston. All rights reserved.

Written Progress Report

OVERALL IMPRESSION

☐ Excellent   ☐ Good   ☐ Satisfactory   ☐ Unsatisfactory

Some particularly good aspects of this item are _____

_____

_____

_____

_____

Some areas that could be improved are _____

_____

_____

_____

_____

To improve your written work, I recommend _____

_____

_____

_____

_____

Additional Comments _____

_____

_____

_____

_____

Copyright © by Holt, Rinehart and Winston. All rights reserved.

Peer Editing Rubric

Chapter _____

I. **Content:** Look for the following elements in your partner's composition. Put a check next to each category when you finish it.

1. _____ Vocabulary

Does the composition use enough new vocabulary from the chapter? Underline all the new vocabulary words you find from this chapter. What additional words do you suggest that your partner try to use?

2. _____ Organization

Is the composition organized and easy to follow? Can you find an introduction and a conclusion?

3. _____ Comprehensibility

Is the composition clear and easy to understand? Is there a specific part that was hard to understand? Did you understand the author's meaning? Draw a box around any sections that were particularly hard to understand.

4. _____ Target Functions and Grammar

Ask your teacher what functions and grammar you should focus on for this chapter and list them below.

Focus: _____

II. **Proofreader's checklist:** Circle any errors you find in your partner's composition so that he or she can correct them. See the chart for some examples.

Incorrect form of the verb	aime J'(aimes) le cinéma.
Adjective – noun agreement Subject – verb agreement	intelligentes Mes amies sont (intelligents). vont Elles (va) à la plage.
Spelling	seize Il a (sieze) ans.
Article	la Il aime (le) glace.
Transition words (if they apply to chapter)	d'abord, ensuite, après, enfin, etc...
Accents and Punctuation	vélo Je fais du (velo).

III. Explain your content and grammar suggestions to your partner. Answer any questions about your comments.

Peer editor's signature: _____ Date: _____

Copyright © by Holt, Rinehart and Winston. All rights reserved.

Portfolio Suggestions

Documentation of Group Work

Item _____ Chapter _____

Group Members: _____

_____

_____

_____

Description of Item: _____

_____

_____

_____

_____

_____

_____

_____

_____

Personal Contribution: _____

_____

_____

_____

_____

_____

_____

_____

_____

_____

_____

Please rate your personal contribution to the group's work.

☐ Excellent ☐ Good ☐ Satisfactory ☐ Unsatisfactory

Copyright © by Holt, Rinehart and Winston. All rights reserved.

Student's Portfolio Checklist

To the Student This form should be used to keep track of the materials you are including in your portfolio. It is important that you keep this list up-to-date so that your portfolio will be complete at the end of the assessment period. As you build your portfolio, try to include pieces of your work that show progress in your ability to speak and write French.

	Type of Item	Date Completed	Date Placed in Portfolio
Item #1			
Item #2			
Item #3			
Item #4			
Item #5			
Item #6			
Item #7			
Item #8			
Item #9			
Item #10			
Item #11			
Item #12			

Copyright © by Holt, Rinehart and Winston. All rights reserved.

Teacher's Portfolio Checklist

To the Teacher This form should be used to keep track of the materials you expect your students to keep in their portfolios for the semester. Encourage students to keep their lists up-to-date so that their portfolios will be complete at the end of the assessment period.

	Type of Item	Date Assigned	Date Due in Portfolio
Item #1			
Item #2			
Item #3			
Item #4			
Item #5			
Item #6			
Item #7			
Item #8			
Item #9			
Item #10			
Item #11			
Item #12			

Copyright © by Holt, Rinehart and Winston. All rights reserved.

Portfolio Self-Evaluation

To the Student Your portfolio consists of selections of your written and oral work. You should consider all the items in your portfolio as you evaluate your progress. Read the statements below and mark a box to the right of each statement to show how well you think your portfolio demonstrates your skills and abilities in French.

	Strongly Agree	Agree	Disagree	Strongly Disagree
1. My portfolio contains all the required items.				
2. My portfolio provides evidence of my progress in speaking and writing French.				
3. The items in my portfolio demonstrate that I can communicate my ideas in French.				
4. The items in my portfolio demonstrate accurate use of French.				
5. The items in my portfolio show that I understand and can use a wide variety of vocabulary.				
6. When I created the items in my portfolio, I tried to use what I had learned in new ways.				
7. The items in my portfolio provide an accurate picture of my skills and abilities in French.				

The item I like best in my portfolio is _____

because (please give at least three reasons) _____

_____

_____

_____

_____

_____

_____

_____

I find my portfolio to be (check one):

☐ Excellent   ☐ Good   ☐ Satisfactory   ☐ Unsatisfactory

Copyright © by Holt, Rinehart and Winston. All rights reserved.

Portfolio Evaluation

To the Student I have reviewed the items in your portfolio and want to share with you my reactions to your work.

Teacher's Signature _____

Date _____

	Strongly Agree	Agree	Disagree	Strongly Disagree
1. Your portfolio contains all the required items.				
2. Your portfolio provides evidence of your progress in speaking and writing French.				
3. The items in your portfolio demonstrate that you can communicate your ideas in French.				
4. The items in your portfolio demonstrate accurate use of French.				
5. The items in your portfolio demonstrate the use of a wide variety of French vocabulary.				
6. The items in your portfolio demonstrate that you have tried to use what you have learned in new ways.				
7. The items in your portfolio provide an accurate picture of your skills and abilities in French.				

The item I like best in your portfolio is _____

because _____

_____

_____

One area in which you seem to need improvement is _____

_____

For your next portfolio collection, I would like to suggest _____

_____

_____

I find your portfolio to be (check one):

☐ Excellent   ☐ Good   ☐ Satisfactory   ☐ Unsatisfactory

Copyright © by Holt, Rinehart and Winston. All rights reserved.

France, les régions

Written: Activity 4

Expanded Activity   Expand Activity 4 by having Martine reply to the letter students wrote about their own school lunch. In the reply, Martine should express happiness at hearing from her pen pal again, comment on the school cafeteria food, and describe her summer vacation: where she went, with whom, what she did, and whether or not she enjoyed it.

Purpose   to renew old acquaintances; to inquire; to express enthusiasm and dissatisfaction; to exchange information

Rationale   Students can practice the functional expressions in the chapter and apply them to a real-life situation.

Materials   pencil or pen and paper

Portfolio Item   Students may include drafts of the letter in their portfolios, or you may agree to use just the final version.

Oral: Activity 2

Expanded Activity   Expand this conversation by having it take place among three friends who meet at a café at the end of the first day of school. Before they talk about their vacations, have them discuss the menu and place their order. While they wait for their food, they tell each other about their recent vacation activities.

Purpose   to inquire; to express enthusiasm and dissatisfaction; to make recommendations; to express indecision; to order and ask for details

Rationale   Applying the targeted expressions to a real-life situation helps students realize that they are learning language for communication.

Materials   small tables and three chairs for each table; posterboard for menus; plates; glasses; silverware; perhaps easily prepared food to be served; audio or video recorder and player; individual cassettes

Portfolio Item   Have students record the conversation at their table at the café and make a copy of it to include in their portfolios.

Copyright © by Holt, Rinehart and Winston. All rights reserved.

Written: Activity 2

Expanded Activity Have students write a letter to Marie-Céline. In addition to answering Marie-Céline's questions, students describe in detail a comic strip or comic book that they really like and one that they really dislike. In each case, students should describe in detail the main characters and the situations these characters encounter. Students should express their enthusiasm for their favorite and their boredom with the other, using appropriate expressions from the chapter. If some students read novels more than comics, they should follow the same procedure, substituting their favorite and least favorite book.

Purpose to express enthusiasm and boredom

Rationale Language learning is more enjoyable to students when they're expressing their personal opinions and feelings.

Materials pencil or pen and paper

Portfolio Item All drafts of the letter should be included in students' portfolios.

Oral: Activity 5

Expanded Activity Have students role-play the following situation: Your friend from the United States is visiting you in Brussels for the weekend. He or she has never been to Brussels, and you want to show not only the famous sights, but also things you like. Partners should create a conversation in which the host first finds out if the guest knows anything about the city. The host then suggests various activities. The guest accepts the ones that interest him or her and rejects the others. Once they have agreed, the guest should express impatience to get started and the host should reassure him or her that there's no hurry.

Purpose to make, accept, and refuse suggestions; to express enthusiasm and boredom; to express impatience; to reassure someone

Rationale Students gain skills that will be helpful to them as future travelers in francophone countries.

Materials audio or video recorder and player; individual cassettes

Portfolio Item The conversation should be recorded and a copy should be included in each student's portfolio.

Copyright © by Holt, Rinehart and Winston. All rights reserved.

3 Soyons responsables!

Written: Activity 4

Expanded Activity Students might work together in small groups to use what they have learned about the environment to write and illustrate a children's fable, the moral of which concerns the protection of the environment. They should create two main characters, one who is insensitive to environmental concerns and another who is very concerned. They should illustrate the book with drawings, magazine cut-outs, or photos that will help convey the message.

Purpose to tell a story; to persuade

Rationale Students will use their French in a creative way. They will also practice organizing their thoughts and relating a series of events.

Materials pencil or pen and paper

Portfolio Item All drafts of the fable should be included in students' portfolios.

Oral: Activity 2

Expanded Activity The class should create a list of activities that require parental permission, such as going to a concert, staying out past a curfew, spending the night at someone's house, and so on. All the suggestions should be written on the board. Have students work in groups of three. Each group should act out one of the scenarios. The teenager should ask his or her parents' permission to do the activity and give a convincing reason why he or she should be allowed to do it. The parents might raise objections or set conditions for their approval, such as returning at a certain hour or doing specific chores. The teenager and the parents should negotiate until they can all agree. Have students change roles so that everyone has a chance to be the teenager. Groups might create a follow-up conversation in which the teenager violates the conditions set by the parents, tries to explain, and is reproached and possibly "grounded."

Purpose to ask for, grant, and refuse permission; to express obligation; to forbid; to reproach; to justify actions and reject excuses

Rationale Giving students an opportunity to practice language in a real-life situation will help them internalize the functional expressions and vocabulary required by the situation.

Materials audio or video recorder and player; individual cassettes

Portfolio Item Record the conversations and have students make a copy to be included in their portfolios.

Copyright © by Holt, Rinehart and Winston. All rights reserved.

Des goûts et des couleurs

Written: Activity 2

Expanded Activity Have students imagine they work for a French fashion magazine. Their assignment is to interview an American teenager about the latest fashions among young people in the United States and also to interview an adult about the reaction of the older generation to the new styles. Students might work in groups of three: the interviewer, the teenager, and the adult. They should work together to prepare a list of questions for the interview. To answer the questions, the teenager describes the various styles favored by young people, and the adult expresses favorable and unfavorable opinions of the different styles. When the interview is over, group members should combine their efforts to write an article for the French magazine relating the interviewer's findings.

Purpose to ask for and give information; to ask for and give opinions

Rationale Interviewing techniques are very important to language learning. Students learn to listen and take notes at the same time.

Materials pencil or pen and paper

Portfolio Items The questionnaire and all drafts of the article should be included in each student's portfolio.

Oral: Activity 3

Expanded Activity Students imagine a situation in which they think their partner might find himself or herself—at a job interview, on a cruise ship, in the mountains, at a wedding, and so on—and make a drawing to illustrate the situation. One partner shows the other his or her picture. The other partner draws and describes what he or she chooses to wear in that situation. The first partner either agrees with and compliments the choice, reassuring the other, or disagrees with the choice and identifies other possibilities (**Tu aurais dû mettre...**). Partners take turns. They might draw more than one situation.

Purpose to ask for and give opinions; to pay and respond to compliments; to reassure someone

Rationale Students will enjoy imagining themselves in other situations. Students need practice in speaking extemporaneously.

Materials pencil or pen and paper; audio or video recorder and player; individual cassettes

Portfolio Item Record the activity and have students make a copy for inclusion in their oral portfolio.

Copyright © by Holt, Rinehart and Winston. All rights reserved.

C'est notre avenir

Written: Activity 30

Expanded Activity Have students write a possible response from a university or school official. In the letter, they should react to the student's letter, provide any additional information the student might need to know, and suggest a date when the student could come to the school or university for an interview.

Purpose to express intentions; to express conditions and possibilities; to express wishes; to write a formal letter

Rationale Responding to interview questions and writing a formal letter simulate real-life tasks that are meaningful to the students' lives.

Materials pencil or pen and paper

Portfolio Items The interview questions and answers and all drafts of the letter should be included in the students' portfolio.

Oral: Activity 25

Expanded Activity To expand and personalize this activity, have students work with a partner who will pretend to be their guidance counselor. Each student should tell the counselor about his or her goals and plans for the future, and the counselor gives advice about how those goals and plans can best be achieved. Students should include in their discussion career possibilities and the conditions they need to meet to get these positions and any practical problems they have to solve.

Purpose to express conditions and possibilities; to ask about and discuss future plans; to express wishes; to ask for and give advice; to request information

Rationale Personalizing the vocabulary and functional expressions will help students remember them longer.

Materials audio or video recorder and player; individual cassettes

Portfolio Item Record the conversation and have students make a copy to include in their portfolios.

Copyright © by Holt, Rinehart and Winston. All rights reserved.

Written: Activity 5

Expanded Activity Have students expand the letter they are writing to their Moroccan pen pal. They should begin the letter by apologizing for not having written sooner. They should add some suggestions as to what they might do during their guest's visit. Before they close, they should make arrangements to meet their guest at the airport. Finally, they should apologize again for having to end the letter because their sister or brother is pestering them to do something or go somewhere; they should complain about their sibling and close the letter.

Purpose to apologize; to make suggestions; to explain hospitality; to make arrangements

Rationale Students need to use functions in writing as well as orally.

Materials pencil or pen and paper

Portfolio Item All drafts of the letter should be included in each student's portfolio.

Oral: Activity 34

Expanded Activity Students might begin by enacting the arrival of the babysitter, who is greeted by the parents of the children. The babysitter might apologize for being late. When the children prove to be insufferable, the babysitter might phone the parents to complain about them and to ask for advice. Here again, the babysitter should apologize for interrupting the parents' evening. The parents should make some suggestions as to what the babysitter might do. She should thank them, hang up, and resolve the situation. Of course, the children will accuse the babysitter of being a tattletale!

Purpose to make, accept, and refuse suggestions; to make and accept apologies; to quarrel; to resolve a problem

Rationale Using the language in a realistic situation that many students have encountered makes communication meaningful.

Materials audio or video recorder and player; individual cassettes

Portfolio Item Record the conversations and have students make a copy for their portfolios.

Copyright © by Holt, Rinehart and Winston. All rights reserved.

PORTFOLIO SUGGESTIONS

Written: Activity 5

Expanded Activity Have students write their adventures as the script of a play. They might first write a list of characters and their descriptions, then add lines for a possible narrator, include stage directions, and finally imagine and describe stage settings. Students may wish to work in small groups to write their scripts. Groups could exchange scripts for editing.

Purpose to make suppositions; to express doubt and certainty; to ask for and give advice; to express astonishment; to caution someone

Rationale Telling a story through dialogue will challenge students to use the language creatively.

Materials pencil or pen and paper

Portfolio Item All drafts of the play should be included in students' portfolios.

Oral: Activity 4

Expanded Activity Have students imagine that they just returned from an African safari and that they have been asked to speak to a group of business people who plan to go on a safari in a few weeks. They should share their experiences, both good and bad, and tell the business people what to expect and what they should take along.

Purpose to ask for and give advice; to caution and reassure someone; to talk about African animals and packing for a safari

Rationale Students gain practice in explaining and describing things.

Materials audio or video player and recorder; individual cassettes

Portfolio Item Record each student's presentation and have them make a copy for their portfolios.

Copyright © by Holt, Rinehart and Winston. All rights reserved.

La Tunisie, pays de contrastes

Written: Activity 18

Expanded Activity Tell students they're exchanging homes and schools with their Tunisian pen pal who lives in Nefta. They've already written a letter to him or her telling about their life in the United States. Have partners exchange letters and answer them, telling what life in Tunisia will be like for the American and what they would like to do in the United States. They should send their best wishes and close the letter appropriately.

Purpose to ask for information; to convey good wishes and information; to give advice; to make cultural comparisons; to close a letter

Rationale Students will enjoy writing from a different perspective.

Materials pencil or pen and paper

Portfolio Item All drafts of the letters should be included in students' portfolios.

Oral: Activity 2

Expanded Activity Students might reverse the situation. They should imagine that they are Tunisians and have been sent information, similar to that on Tunis and Tozeur, about two possible places to live in the United States, one a big city, the other a small town. In preparation for the activity, students might suggest a city and a small town in their state or elsewhere and note some features of each place to use in their conversation about the pros and cons of living in each location.

Purpose to make comparisons; to express wishes; to give advice

Rationale Students will expand their knowledge of their own region or country by comparing various locations.

Materials audio or video recorder and player; individual cassettes

Portfolio Item Have students record the conversations and include a copy in their portfolios.

Copyright © by Holt, Rinehart and Winston. All rights reserved.

Written: Activity 5

Expanded Activity Have students write a letter to their pen pal in which they describe a movie they really disliked. They should describe the plot and any features of the film that they didn't like (acting, directing, special effects, and so on). They should advise their pen pal not to see it.

Purpose to make judgments; to summarize a story; to make recommendations

Rationale Having students cite examples to clarify an opinion is a valuable skill in any language.

Materials pencil or pen and paper

Portfolio Item All drafts of the letter should be included in students' portfolios.

Oral: Activity 4

Expanded Activity Have partners expand or vary this activity to discuss TV stars and shows. They should imagine they are outside the theater where the Emmy awards are being given. As they watch the TV stars enter, they comment on their favorite shows. Each partner should try to convince the other to watch a show. They should take turns suggesting shows to watch and not to watch.

Purpose to agree and disagree; to ask for and make judgments and recommendations

Rationale Using new expressions to communicate real information about a subject that is relevant to students increases their motivation.

Materials audio or video recorder and player; individual cassettes

Portfolio Item Record the conversation and have students copy it onto their personal cassettes.

Copyright © by Holt, Rinehart and Winston. All rights reserved.

Rencontres au soleil

P O R T F O L I O   S U G G E S T I O N S

Portfolio Suggestions

Written: Activity 32

Expanded Activity Have students exchange the notes they have written and write a reply directly to Eric, commenting on some of the things that happened to him. Since Eric is a friend, they should feel comfortable teasing him a little about his misfortunes! In their response, they should brag about some of the interesting things that have happened to them lately, even if they have to exaggerate a little, but should also mention one or two not so pleasant things that have happened.

Purpose to describe past events; to flatter; to brag; to tease

Rationale Students can have fun with the language by bragging, exaggerating, and teasing a friend.

Materials pencil or pen and paper

Portfolio Item All drafts of the original letter and the reply should be included in students' portfolios.

Oral: Activity 4

Expanded Activity After the partners have boasted to each other of their accomplishment(s), have them phone a friend and relate what their partner said. They should express their disbelief at what their partner said or their admiration for their partner's accomplishment(s). The friend should react with interest or with disbelief. The partners should play the role of each other's friend in the phone conversations.

Purpose to break some news; to show interest; to express disbelief

Rationale Paraphrasing is a useful skill.

Materials audio or video recorder and player; individual cassettes

Portfolio Item Students should record the conversation on their personal cassettes and add them to their portfolios.

Copyright © by Holt, Rinehart and Winston. All rights reserved.

CHAPITRE 11 Laissez les bons temps rouler!

Written: Activity 5

Expanded Activity To expand this activity, have groups of students use the articles they wrote about Louisiana to prepare a script for a 30-second TV commercial about Louisiana. They might choose one aspect of Cajun life or incorporate various aspects mentioned in their articles. The group should compose a slogan as the title of their commercial that would attract visitors to Louisiana. The commercial could involve a narration with pictures or interviews with local inhabitants. If resources permit, groups might videotape their commercials.

Purpose to make observations about another culture; to give information; to describe places visited

Rationale Using French to communicate real information is very motivating for students.

Materials pencil or pen and paper; magazines; travel brochures

Portfolio Item All drafts of the script should be included in each student's portfolio.

Oral: Activity 17

Expanded Activity In small groups, students imagine they're VJ's for a French music show for teenagers that introduces all the hit songs. They should give their opinions about songs and singers, talk about the latest stars of rock, country, zydeco, jazz, pop, blues, etc., agree and disagree with each other, and rate songs. Students might videotape this activity.

Purpose to make observations; to give impressions; to give opinions; to agree and disagree

Rationale By applying the targeted functional expressions to a real-life situation, students learn to communicate more easily.

Materials photos or pictures of Louisiana; audio or video recorder and player; individual cassettes

Portfolio Item Have students record their shows on their personal cassettes for their portfolios.

Copyright © by Holt, Rinehart and Winston. All rights reserved.

Echanges sportifs et culturels

Written: Activity 4

Expanded Activity Tell students they won the trip to the Olympic Games as a result of their essay. They should imagine they are at the Games and write a letter to their French class. In their letter they should answer the following questions: What have you seen so far? Who won and lost? Were there any surprises? Any disappointments? Did you make the right decision about which events to see? What event(s) are you going to see? What do you think the outcome will be? What have you been doing other than attending events? Are you enjoying the locale and the food? Have you met new friends? What have you learned?

Purpose to relate past events; to express excitement and disappointment; to express certainty and doubt

Rationale Imaginative, creative use of the language that goes beyond the everyday use of French is enjoyable and motivating for students.

Materials pencil or pen and paper

Portfolio Item All drafts of the letter should be included in students' portfolios.

Oral: Activity 3

Expanded Activity Have students imagine they are now at the Games and are being interviewed by a francophone TV reporter. Students might use the letter suggested in the written activity above as the basis of the interview. The interviewer could use the same questions in French. In the course of the interview, the student should mention how he or she won a trip to the Olympics by winning an essay contest. Students should record their interviews.

Purpose to inquire; to express anticipation, certainty, and doubt; to express excitement and disappointment

Rationale Students practice asking and answering questions in a creative context.

Materials audio or video recorder and player; individual cassettes

Portfolio Item Students should record the interview and include their cassettes in their portfolios.

Copyright © by Holt, Rinehart and Winston. All rights reserved.

Performance Assessment

France, les régions

Première étape

In groups of three or four, have students act out a scene similar to **Les Retrouvailles,** the scene in the Chapter 1 **Mise en train** where several friends meet at the end of summer. Have them greet one another and ask about one another's vacation. You might have groups turn in their written scripts.

Deuxième étape

Have students pretend that they are restaurant critics who will be featured on a special television promotion for restaurants in their city. They should each choose a restaurant and give a positive critique of it for the television audience (the class), using the vocabulary on page 31 of the *Pupil's Edition.* Have them also recommend dishes to try.

Global Performance Assessment

Have students act out a scene at a restaurant with friends. One student plays the server. The others, playing the customers, look at the menu from Le Cygne, but are unsure about what to order. Have students ask each other questions, make recommendations, and order.

PERFORMANCE ASSESSMENT

Copyright © by Holt, Rinehart and Winston. All rights reserved.

Belgique, nous voilà!

Première étape

On a transparency, draw a map that includes several different highways, a bridge, several cities or towns, and some intersections. Label the towns and highways, using Belgian designations. (See Culture Note on page 35 of the *Teacher's Edition.*) Then play the role of a lost motorist and ask students how to get to various cities from a specified point.

Deuxième étape

Have groups of three or four students create a skit in which they visit the **Centre de la BD** and shop for a gift for a friend's birthday. Students should ask for directions to several places in the museum, including the gift store, and they should discuss and give one another their opinions of various comic books they're considering buying for their friend.

Global Performance Assessment

Have students act out the following situation with a partner. One student has selected one of the destinations on page 59 of the *Pupil's Edition* to visit, but doesn't know how to get there. He or she must call the tourist bureau to ask where the town is and how to get there from Stavelot, write the directions, and repeat them to make sure they're correct. The student playing the role of the tourist bureau employee can use the map on page 38 of the *Pupil's Edition* to give directions.

Copyright © by Holt, Rinehart and Winston. All rights reserved.

Soyons responsables!

Première étape

Write the different rooms or areas of the house on index cards. Have students choose a card and tell a friend three chores that they both need to do in that room before going out. The friend might protest, but the student should be firm.

Deuxième étape

Distribute an equal number of squares of green and blue construction paper. Each "green" pairs up with a "blue" and they act out a brief skit in which the "green" reprimands the "blue" for irresponsible behavior and gives advice on how to be more considerate or environmentally conscious. The "blue" may choose to be receptive or to protest and make excuses. The "green" should reject any excuses for inappropriate behavior.

Global Performance Assessment

Have students work in groups to make preparations to participate in a demonstration. First they should choose a good cause, such as forest conservation, animal protection, or water and air pollution. Then they should make signs with slogans and plan what they're going to say to the crowd of onlookers. Have them act out this scene. The rest of the class will act as onlookers who aren't very interested in the environment. The group of presenters should remind the onlookers of their obligations.

Copyright © by Holt, Rinehart and Winston. All rights reserved.

Des goûts et des couleurs

Première étape

Have partners act out a skit about two friends in a clothing store. One tries on bizarre combinations of clothing (striped pants with a plaid shirt) and asks for opinions of them. The other compliments the outfits, but makes suggestions for other choices (a white shirt with striped pants).

Deuxième étape

Have partners create and act out a skit in which two friends choose new outfits and hairstyles for a special event (a concert, a family reunion, a school dance). They should ask for and give opinions about various clothing and hair styles, as well as compliment and reassure each other on their final choices.

Global Performance Assessment

Have students work in groups to create outfits to present in a fashion show. Each student should make sketches of outfits and ask the other group members their opinions. Then the group decides together which outfits they're going to present and write descriptions of them. During the fashion show, students should take turns being models and the commentator who describes the clothing. As the audience, the rest of the class will point out the outfits that they find interesting and tell what they think of them. They'll also write down their opinions of each outfit. After the show, have students tell which outfits are the most popular.

PERFORMANCE ASSESSMENT

Copyright © by Holt, Rinehart and Winston. All rights reserved.

C'est notre avenir

Première étape

Have students find their partners from Activity 13 on page 135 of the *Pupil's Edition* and act out one of the conversations from that activity.

Deuxième étape

Have students create and act out a conversation between two indecisive friends who are trying to decide what to do in the future. Challenge students to use as many of the chapter functions as possible in their conversations. You might even award a point for each function or vocabulary item used and offer a small prize to the pair with the most points.

Global Performance Assessment

Have students work in pairs to act out a scene between a parent and a teenager. The teenager talks to his or her parent about what he or she is thinking of doing after high school, what he or she wants to do with in the future, and why. The parent is not very happy with this choice and tries to discourage the teenager from it. The teenager tries to convince the parent. Have students change roles.

Copyright © by Holt, Rinehart and Winston. All rights reserved.

Ma famille, mes copains et moi

Première étape

Have groups of three write and act out a conversation in a market in which one student sells pottery, one sells mint tea at a stand, and the other is a new vendor who sells carpets. In the scene, students should introduce themselves, make suggestions about things to do, and arrange to meet later.

Deuxième étape

Have students act out the skits they created for Activity 34 in the *Pupil's Edition*. You might suggest that the guests take on the roles of celebrities who are known for not getting along well together. You might also videotape or record students' skits. Base students' grades on vocabulary use, creativity, pronunciation, and presentation.

Global Performance Assessment

Have students act out the following scenes with their classmates. They're going to their cousin's wedding.

- When they arrive at their cousin's house, the family offers greetings and tries to make them feel at home.
- The night before the wedding, their cousin's fiancé(e) shows up looking angry. The engaged couple has a quarrel. They make up, however, and apologize to each other and to their guests.
- On the day of the wedding, there are some family members attending whom the student doesn't know. Their cousin explains who they are and introduces everyone.

Copyright © by Holt, Rinehart and Winston. All rights reserved.

Un safari-photo

PERFORMANCE ASSESSMENT

Première étape

Have students act out their skits from Part b of Activity 16 on page 196 of the *Pupil's Edition*. Encourage them to use props and to offer explanations for the advice they give.

Deuxième étape

Assign five words or expressions from the vocabulary list on page 215 of the *Pupil's Edition* to each of several small groups. Give groups two or three minutes to create a brief conversation, using the assigned vocabulary. Call on groups to present their skits to the class. After a group has performed, have the class identify and write down the vocabulary words and expressions from this chapter the group used.

Global Performance Assessment

Have students act out a scene where several people are camping in a reserve. Suddenly they hear noises that sound like gunshots. Wondering what the noises could be, the group decides to go see what's happening. As they come over a hill, they see poachers. Knowing that they could be in danger, they leave immediately. When they reach a village, they look for a phone to call the reserve patrol. Students should remember to do the following things at the appropriate times:

- express fear
- warn their friends
- make suppositions
- reassure one another
- express their relief

Copyright © by Holt, Rinehart and Winston. All rights reserved.

La Tunisie, pays de contrastes

Première étape

On separate index cards, write the expressions for asking someone to convey good wishes, expressing hope or wishes, and giving advice. Have partners draw two cards each and then create and act out a brief skit, logically incorporating all four expressions.

Deuxième étape

Write **en ville** or **à la campagne** on cards and put them in a bag. Have partners draw a card and create a conversation about living in the area written on their card. They might agree or disagree with each other. Have them present their conversation to the class.

Global Performance Assessment

Have students pair off to act out the following situation. One student is visiting a friend (his or her partner) who lives in a very big city. The friend want to show off one of the city's famous attractions.

- On the way, there is a big traffic jam. It's very hot and both friends are very unhappy. They complain about the situation.

- The friends finally arrive at their destination, but someone zooms in front of the car into the last parking space. They express their annoyance.

- The two friends stand in line to get tickets and someone cuts in front of them. They're both furious.

- Finally the friends get out of the car to go in, but a few minutes later, someone announces that the attraction is about to close. Now they've really had it!

Copyright © by Holt, Rinehart and Winston. All rights reserved.

PERFORMANCE ASSESSMENT

C'est l'fun!

Première étape

Have students perform their skits from Activity 19 on page 260 of the *Pupil's Edition*. If possible, provide a television, a remote control, and a TV program guide for students to use as props.

Deuxième étape

Have partners critique three movies. One student should summarize the movie's plot and give his or her opinion, using the thumbs-up or the thumbs-down gesture for the final evaluation. The other student should either agree or disagree and give a final recommendation as well.

Global Performance Assessment

Have students imagine they're journalists at the **Festival des Films du monde** in Montreal. They're going to interview a star. The star will tell about a new movie he/she has just made—what kind of movie it is, what it's about, what other actors/actresses are in it, and what he/she thinks about it. Students should remember to ask his/her opinion about other movies at the festival. They should act out this scene with a classmate and then change roles.

Copyright © by Holt, Rinehart and Winston. All rights reserved.

Rencontres au soleil

Première étape

Write on index cards the situations students suggested for the Motivating Activity in the top left column of page 290 of the *Annotated Teacher's Edition.* Have partners draw a card and act out a brief skit in which one student teases the other. You might base students' grades on inclusion of all the elements, language use, creativity, and participation.

Deuxième étape

Have students perform their scenes from Activity 36 on page 297 of the *Pupil's Edition.*

Global Performance Assessment

Have students act out having a party in honor of one student's pen pal from Guadeloupe, who is visiting. At the party, they'll break some news, tell jokes, brag, flatter, and tease each other. Students should form groups to write out a script of this scene and act it out. They should include the following situations.

- Each student makes up two bits of news to tell the others.
- The pen pal talks about what it's like in Guadeloupe. He/She makes up an event to brag about. The others flatter him/her.
- Each student teases one of their friends.

PERFORMANCE ASSESSMENT

Copyright © by Holt, Rinehart and Winston. All rights reserved.

Première étape

Form small groups. Have students take on the identity of various musicians and exchange opinions of various types of music, according to their new identity.

Deuxième étape

Have students perform their skits from Activity 28 on page 325 of the *Pupil's Edition*. You might videotape their performances.

Global Performance Assessment

Have students imagine they're visiting friends in southern Louisiana. They are taken to a Cajun restaurant and dance hall. They should act out the following scenes with their classmates.

a. The visitor doesn't know what to order, so the friends make suggestions. Because the visitor isn't familiar with the suggested foods, he or she asks for some explanation. The visitor tastes the food, and the friends want to know what he or she thinks. The visitor should give an opinion and add an observation about Cajun food.

b. At the dance hall, the friends discuss music preferences. A live band starts to play. The visitor doesn't know what kind of music it is, so he or she asks the friends. They explain what kind of music it is, and then ask for the visitor's reaction to both the music and the dancing. The visitor should give his or her impressions.

PERFORMANCE ASSESSMENT

Copyright © by Holt, Rinehart and Winston. All rights reserved.

12 Echanges sportifs et culturels

Première étape

Have partners role-play an interview with an athlete's proud parent just after the athlete has left for the Olympic Games.

Deuxième étape

Have students choose a country and research a few facts about it before class. Then have two students sit at the front of the classroom. One student plays the role of a sports journalist and the other, the role of an athlete from the country he or she selected. Have the journalist ask the athlete questions about his or her country and the athlete respond without naming it. The first student in the class to guess which country the athlete is from takes the next turn and chooses his or her journalist.

Global Performance Assessment

Have students work in pairs. Both partners are Olympic athletes. They choose the sports that they play and the countries they represent. Then they should act out the following situations.

a. The athletes are meeting each other in the Olympic village for the first time. They ask questions to find out about each other's country and interests.

b. They meet again on the last day. They tell each other how their competitions went. (One did very well and one did poorly.) They talk about their other experiences and what they've enjoyed about the Games.

Copyright © by Holt, Rinehart and Winston. All rights reserved.

Using CD-ROM
for Assessment

Guided Recording

A toi de parler

Students record a conversation between a restaurant server and a customer based on the following prompts:

CUSTOMER Tell the server that you're having trouble deciding what to order.

SERVER Suggest a main dish for the customer to try.

CUSTOMER Ask what is in the main dish the server suggests.

SERVER Describe the main dish the customer asks about.

CUSTOMER Order a main dish, an appetizer, and a beverage.

Guided Writing

A toi d'écrire

Students choose from among the following four writing scenarios.

 Conversation Ecris une conversation de 8 à 10 lignes entre un(e) invité(e) qui arrive à Paris après un long voyage et son ami(e). L'ami(e) doit saluer son invité(e) et lui poser au moins trois questions sur son voyage.

 Enquête Ton oncle et ta tante vont ouvrir un nouveau restaurant en France et tu vas les aider. Ecris un questionnaire de 8 ou 10 questions dans lequel tu demandes aux gens ce qu'ils pensent de certains plats et quelles sont leurs préférences pour chaque catégorie : entrée, plat principal et dessert.

 Journal Les vacances d'été les plus mémorables de ta vie sont terminées. Tu ne veux jamais les oublier, alors tu les racontes dans ton journal. Dis avec le plus de détails possible où tu es allé(e), ce que tu as fait et ce que tu as vu.

 Menu Ecris un menu pour un nouveau restaurant. Donne trois ou quatre choix pour chaque catégorie. Fais attention de donner beaucoup de choix pour que le restaurant attire une grande variété de clients.

Copyright © by Holt, Rinehart and Winston. All rights reserved.

Belgique, nous voilà!

Guided Recording

A toi de parler

Students record a conversation between a gas station attendant and a customer based on the following prompts:

ETUDIANT(E) A Ask your partner to fill up your car.

ETUDIANT(E) B Ask your partner if you should check the oil.

ETUDIANT(E) A Respond positively to your partner's question and ask him or her to clean the windshield as well.

ETUDIANT(E) B Tell your partner that you need to put oil in the motor.

ETUDIANT(E) A Ask your partner to put air in the tires also.

Guided Writing

A toi d'écrire

Students choose from among the following four writing scenarios. The first topic emphasizes the writing process.

 Article Tu es reporter pour un magazine de tourisme. Ta mission est d'écrire un article de 10 à 12 lignes sur les principales attractions de la Belgique.

 Lettre Ecris une lettre à ton correspondant français pour lui parler de tes bandes des-sinées préférées. Décris les personnages en détail et explique pourquoi tu les aimes. Tu peux aussi parler de bandes dessinées que tu n'aimes pas.

 Script Ecris une scène de 10 à 12 lignes pour une comédie. Ton personnage principal a un rendez-vous très important mais il ne sait pas comment y arriver. Il demande sa route à des gens qui lui donnent des explications très compliquées.

 Script Tu es dessinateur de bande dessinées. Tu dois écrire un dialogue pour un épisode humoristique qui se passe dans une station-service. Juste avant de partir pour un long voyage en voiture, ton personnage principal donne à son ami, le pompiste de la station-service, des instructions pour faire la révision de sa voiture. Le pompiste n'est pas très rapide et le client s'impatiente. Une fois que tu as écrit ton dialogue, tu peux créer ta bande dessinée et coller ton dialogue dans tes bulles, sur ton dessin.

Have students follow these steps to complete their article.

PRELIMINAIRES Fais une liste des sites, attractions et spécialités belges que tu connais. Pour faire ta recherche, tu peux utiliser tes livres de français, une encyclopédie ou Internet.

REDACTION Commence par une introduction sur la Belgique : sur quel continent elle se trouve, quelles langues on y parle et d'autres faits généraux. Ensuite, choisis quelques idées dans tes PRELIMINAIRES et présente-les dans ton article. Conclus avec une phrase qui résume tes idées et qui explique pourquoi tu conseilles aux lecteurs de visiter la Belgique.

RELECTURE Imprime ton article, relis-le et fais les changements nécessaires. N'oublie pas de vérifier l'orthographe, les accents et les majuscules.

PUBLICATION Imprime une copie finale de ton article.

Copyright © by Holt, Rinehart and Winston. All rights reserved.

Soyons responsables!

CD-ROM Assessment

Guided Recording

A toi de parler

Students record a conversation between a mother and a son based on the following prompts:

LE FILS Ask your mother's permission to go to your friend's house.

LA MERE Tell your son to water the yard first.

LE FILS Ask your mother's permission to go to a movie tonight.

LA MERE Tell your son OK, just this once.

LE FILS Tell your mother you'll wash the windows tomorrow.

LA MERE Tell your son to be polite with his friend's parents.

Guided Writing

A toi d'écrire

Students choose from among the following four writing scenarios. The third topic emphasizes the writing process.

 Poster Tu es moniteur ou monitrice dans une colonie de vacances. Tu veux que les jeunes de ta colonie apprennent à être responsables en société et dans la nature. Ecris le texte d'une affiche avec dix à douze recommandations à faire à tes jeunes.

 Article Ecris un article de journal sur la protection de l'environnement.

 Enquête Tu fais une enquête parmi les jeunes de ton école au sujet de leurs responsabilités ménagères. Prépare dix à douze questions précises. Ils doivent y répondre par «oui» ou par «non».

 Lettre Tu veux travailler au pair dans une famille française pendant l'été. Ecris une lettre à la famille que tu as choisie. Explique-lui pourquoi tu veux travailler en France. Fais la liste de ce que tu sais faire à la maison et demande une description de ton travail dans la famille.

Have students follow these steps to complete their article.

REDACTION Commence par une introduction où tu expliques pourquoi la protection de l'environnement est importante pour la société. Ensuite, décris en huit à dix lignes les différentes initiatives qu'on peut prendre pour protéger l'environnement. Finalement, dis comment tu vois le futur de notre planète.

RELECTURE Imprime ton article, relis-le et fais les changements nécessaires. N'oublie pas de vérifier l'orthographe, les accents et les majuscules.

PUBLICATION Imprime une copie finale de ton article.

Copyright © by Holt, Rinehart and Winston. All rights reserved.

Des goûts et des couleurs

Guided Recording

A toi de parler

Students record four conversations based on several illustrations and the following prompts:

ELEVE 1 Demande à ton/ta camarade ce qu'il/elle pense de l'article montré sur l'illustration 1.

ELEVE 2 Donne ton opinion sur l'article à ton/ta camarade.

ELEVE 1 Demande à ton/ta camarade ce qu'il/elle pense de l'article montré sur l'illustration 2.

ELEVE 2 Donne ton opinion sur l'article à ton/ta camarade.

ELEVE 1 Demande à ton/ta camarade ce qu'il/elle pense de l'article montré sur l'illustration 3.

ELEVE 2 Donne ton opinion sur l'article à ton/ta camarade.

ELEVE 1 Demande à ton/ta camarade ce qu'il/elle pense de l'article montré sur l'illustration 4.

ELEVE 2 Donne ton opinion sur l'article à ton/ta camarade.

Guided Writing

A toi d'écrire

Students choose from among the following four writing scenarios.

 Reportage Tu dois faire un reportage télévisé sur une nouvelle collection de mode pour le printemps. Prépare ton reportage. Décris le type, le style et la couleur de chaque vêtement de la collection.

 Conversation Tu vas dans un magasin avec un(e) ami(e) pour acheter des vêtements. Vous faites des commentaires sur les vêtements que vous voyez. Le vendeur ou la vendeuse vous fait des suggestions et des compliments. Utilise des pronoms interrogatifs et demontratifs dans ton dialogue.

 Brochure Tu dois préparer une brochure pour un salon de coiffure. Ecris quatre annonces publicitaires qui décrivent des coupes de cheveux différentes, deux pour homme et deux pour femme. Après avoir imprimé ta brochure, tu peux coller des photos pour illustrer chaque style de coiffure.

 Liste Tu es très occupé(e) en ce moment. Fais une liste de six ou sept choses que tu dois faire faire (réparations, nettoyage, coiffure, etc.) cette semaine. Fais des phrases complètes.

CD-ROM ASSESSMENT

Copyright © by Holt, Rinehart and Winston. All rights reserved.

C'est notre avenir

Guided Recording

A toi de parler

Students record four short descriptions of a young girl's plans for the future, based on illustrations and the following textual prompts:

PROMPT 1 Qu'est-ce que Bertille fera cet été?

PROMPT 2 Qu'est-ce que Bertille fera après son voyage?

PROMPT 3 Qu'est-ce qu'elle aimerait faire après ses études?

PROMPT 4 Qu'est-ce qu'elle aimerait faire comme métier?

Guided Writing

A toi d'écrire

Students choose from among the following four writing scenarios. The first topic emphasizes the writing process.

 Lettre Tu vas bientôt finir le lycée et tu voudrais avoir des renseignements sur les universités qui t'intéressent.

 Enquête Tu voudrais savoir ce que tes camarades de classe vont faire après le lycée. Ecris un questionnaire de huit à dix questions où tu leur demandes de t'expliquer leurs projets. Tes questions doivent porter sur les études, les métiers et la famille.

 Fax Tu viens de passer un an à Dakar dans une famille sénégalaise. Ta famille d'accueil t'invite à visiter quelques régions du Sénégal pendant deux semaines. Il y a un télécopieur dans le bureau de ton père d'accueil et tu décides d'envoyer un fax à tes parents. Tu leur expliques que tu hésites à partir avec ta famille sénégalaise mais que tu voudrais bien visiter le Sénégal avec elle.

 Courrier électronique Un(e) élève francophone a passé un an dans ton lycée l'année dernière. Maintenant, il/elle est reparti(e) en France. Ecris-lui un courrier électronique de sept ou huit lignes où tu lui poses des questions sur ce qu'il/elle veut faire maintenant. Donne-lui des conseils. Tu peux aussi parler de tes projets personnels.

Have students follow these steps to complete their letter.

PRELIMINAIRES Fais une liste des questions que tu veux poser dans ta lettre à des universités.

REDACTION Ecris une lettre de quatre ou cinq phrases. Utilise ta liste de questions. Donne quelques renseignements sur toi. Parle de tes activités et de tes rêves de carrière. Demande une brochure. Conclus ta lettre avec une formule de politesse.

RELECTURE Imprime ta lettre, relis-la et fais les changements nécessaires. N'oublie pas de vérifier l'orthographe, les accents et les majuscules.

CD-ROM ASSESSMENT

Copyright © by Holt, Rinehart and Winston. All rights reserved.

Ma famille, mes copains et moi

Guided Recording

A toi de parler

Students record a conversation based on the following prompts:

ETUDIANT A Suggest that you meet tomorrow night.

ETUDIANT B Answer yes, and ask how you should work it out.

ETUDIANT A Propose a time and a place to meet.

ETUDIANT B Say that it would be nice, but that you have an appointment at that time.

ETUDIANT A Propose another time.

ETUDIANT B Answer that you'd like that a lot.

Guided Writing

A toi d'écrire

Students choose from among the following four writing scenarios.

 Lettre La semaine dernière, tu es allé(e) à Paris et tu as complètement oublié de rendre visite à ta tante Rosalie. Tu devais lui apporter un cadeau de la part de tes parents. Tu devais aussi l'inviter à dîner et aller au cinéma avec elle. Ecris-lui une lettre pour t'excuser de n'avoir pas fait toutes ces choses.

 Bande dessinée Tu as des frères jumeaux qui se disputent tout le temps. Pour leur anniversaire, tu vas leur préparer une bande dessinée satirique qui illustre une de leurs disputes. Ecris au moins dix répliques pour les bulles de ta bande dessinée.

 Scénario Tu dois écrire une scène pour ta classe de théâtre où un homme reçoit un couple d'amis à dîner. Il accueille ses invités, leur sert à boire; les amis le remercient et l'hôte répond à leurs remerciements. La scène doit avoir sept ou huit répliques.

 Journal Tu ne veux pas oublier ta visite au Maroc dans la famille de ton ami Ali. Il y a huit personnes dans sa famille. Décris-les dans ton journal et dis qui ils sont par rapport à Ali.

Copyright © by Holt, Rinehart and Winston. All rights reserved.

CD-ROM ASSESSMENT

Un safari-photo

CD-ROM Assessment

Guided Recording

A toi de parler

Students record warnings for various people, based on illustrations they see and the following prompts:

PROMPT 1 Dis à Fabien ce qu'il doit faire et pourquoi.

PROMPT 2 Signale à tes amis que les gazelles chargent!

PROMPT 3 Avertis Arnaud qu'il y a des fourmis par terre.

PROMPT 4 Avertis Suzanne qu'il y a un lion derrière elle.

Guided Writing

A toi d'écrire

Students choose from among the following four writing scenarios. The second topic emphasizes the writing process.

 Article Tu fais un safari en Afrique et tu voudrais écrire un article pour le journal de ton école.

 Catalogue Tu viens d'ouvrir un magasin pour les gens qui voyagent à l'étranger. Pour le catalogue de ton magasin, présente les objets nécessaires pour deux voyages : une croisière en Méditerranée et une randonnée en canoë. Nomme chaque objet et donnes-en le prix et une brève description. Laisse de l'espace pour les photos des objets que tu pourras coller après avoir imprimé ta brochure.

 Courrier électronique Tu vas bientôt faire un safari en Afrique. Dis ce que tu penses voir pendant ton safari dans un courrier électronique à ton ami suisse. Imagine ce qui va certainement arriver et ce qui ne va probablement pas arriver. Ajoute quelques phrases sur ce que tu voudrais vraiment faire pendant ton voyage.

 Petit mot Tu viens de recevoir un petit mot d'un ami qui te demande des conseils pour son voyage au Grand Canyon. Il veut savoir ce qu'il doit emporter. Tu connais bien le Grand Canyon et tu fais des recommandations à ton ami dans un mot de sept ou huit phrases.

Have students follow these steps to complete their article.

PRELIMINAIRES Fais une liste de tous les animaux que tu as vus et que tu penses voir pendant ton safari.

REDACTION Ecris un article de sept ou huit phrases dans lequel tu racontes tes aventures. Utilise ta liste des PRELIMINAIRES. Fais aussi des recommandations aux élèves qui voudraient faire un safari.

RELECTURE Imprime ton article, relis-le et fais les changements nécessaires. N'oublie pas de vérifier l'orthographe, les accents et les majuscules.

CD-ROM ASSESSMENT

Copyright © by Holt, Rinehart and Winston. All rights reserved.

CHAPITRE **8**

La Tunisie, pays de contrastes

CD-ROM Assessment

Guided Recording

A toi de parler

Students record their responses to the following questions:

VIDEO 1 Est-ce que tu trouves que la Tunisie est plus moderne ou moins moderne que les Etats-Unis? Explique-moi pourquoi.

VIDEO 2 Est-ce que tu peux me décrire Tunis? Les rues, les gens, la ville en général?

VIDEO 3 Si tu pouvais rester en Tunisie, est-ce que tu irais à l'université ou est-ce que tu aimerais travailler? Pourquoi?

VIDEO 4 Quelles sont les activités traditionnelles des Tunisiens?

VIDEO 5 Si tu travaillais en Tunisie, est-ce que tu aimerais mieux faire la cueillette des dattes ou faire de la poterie? Pourquoi?

Guided Writing

A toi d'écrire

Students choose from among the following four writing scenarios:

 Liste Tu habites avec une famille à Monastir pendant une semaine. Ta mère d'accueil t'a donné une liste de choses à faire pendant qu'elle travaille, mais tu l'as perdue. Refais la liste de choses à acheter au magasin et de choses à faire dans la maison.

 Journal Tu viens d'un petit village et tu passes tes vacances à Tunis. Ecris sept ou huit lignes dans ton journal. Décris la vie à Tunis, ce que tu aimes et ce que tu n'aimes pas là-bas, et explique pourquoi. Compare Tunis à ta ville natale.

 Lettre Tu as passé des vacances dans une famille tunisienne. Ecris une lettre de six ou sept lignes à ta famille d'accueil pour la remercier. N'oublie pas de saluer tout le monde à la fin de ta lettre.

 Lettre Tu as payé ta place de stationnement mais tu as reçu une contravention. Tu penses que ce n'est pas juste et tu es furieux/furieuse. Ecris une lettre de six à sept lignes à la police pour expliquer la situation.

CD-ROM ASSESSMENT

Copyright © by Holt, Rinehart and Winston. All rights reserved.

C'est l'fun!

Guided Recording

A toi de parler

Students record comments about several TV programs based on the following prompts:

PROMPT 1 Dis à ta mère de quel type d'émission il s'agit et comment tu la trouves.

PROMPT 2 Dis à ta mère pourquoi tu trouves cette émission ennuyeuse.

PROMPT 3 Dis à ta mère de quel type de film il s'agit et recommande-le.

PROMPT 4 Explique de quel type d'émission il s'agit et pourquoi tu ne la recommandes pas.

Guided Writing

A toi d'écrire

Students choose from among the following four writing scenarios. The first topic emphasizes the writing process.

 Script Tu es scénariste à Hollywood et tu dois écrire un dialogue entre deux amis qui parlent d'un feuilleton.

 Journal Tu pars en vacances avec des ami(e)s et tu essaies de dormir dans la voiture pendant le voyage. Tout le monde parle fort et écoute de la musique, donc tu es en colère. Plus tard, chez toi, tu écris environ huit lignes dans ton journal à propos de ce qui est arrivé pendant le voyage. Raconte comment tu as demandé à tes amis d'être silencieux et comment ils ont répondu.

 TV Program Tu voudrais te mettre d'accord avec tes frères et sœurs sur ce que vous allez regarder à la télé cette semaine. Ton frère aime seulement les sports et ta sœur ne regarde que les feuilletons. Toi, tu préfères les jeux télévisés et les documentaires. Fais un programme qui inclut les types d'émissions que tout le monde veut voir, le titre de chaque émission et l'heure à laquelle chaque émission passe. Inclus au moins dix émissions.

 Article Fais la critique de deux ou trois films que tu as vus récemment pour le journal de ton école. Parle des acteurs, de l'intrigue et des genres de films dont il s'agit. Finalement, dis si tu recommandes chaque film ou pas, et pourquoi.

Have students follow these steps to complete their script.

PRELIMINAIRES Fais une liste des aspects du feuilleton dont tes personnages vont parler. Inclus le sujet, le lieu de l'action et l'intrigue du feuilleton.

REDACTION Ecris un dialogue de sept ou huit phrases entre les deux amis. Utilise ta liste des PRELIMINAIRES. Décris aussi ce que les deux amis pensent du feuilleton.

RELECTURE Imprime ton dialogue, relis-le et fais les changements nécessaires. N'oublie pas de vérifier l'orthographe, les accents et les majuscules.

Copyright © by Holt, Rinehart and Winston. All rights reserved.

Rencontres au soleil

Guided Recording

A toi de parler

Students record their responses to the following video prompts:

PROMPT 1 J'ai entendu dire que Romain veut se marier avec Pauline. Raconte!

PROMPT 2 Avant mon départ, Lucien et Thérèse avaient eu une dispute. Est-ce que ça va mieux?

PROMPT 3 Michelle avait commencé un régime quand j'étais là-bas. Est-ce qu'elle continue?

PROMPT 4 Didier avait embouti sa nouvelle voiture avant mon départ. Comment va sa jambe?

PROMPT 5 Ma cousine m'avait dit qu'elle voulait apprendre à conduire. Qu'est-ce qu'elle fait en ce moment?

Guided Writing

A toi d'écrire

Students choose from among the following four writing scenarios.

 Petit mot Ton ami Maxime t'a écrit pour te raconter ses aventures de plongée en Tunisie. Ecris-lui un petit mot où tu exprimes ton admiration à propos de ce que Maxime a vu et fait.

 Journal Tes amis te taquinent tout le temps et ça t'énerve! Ecris dans ton journal tout ce qui arrive. Décris en sept ou huit lignes une conversation entre tes amis et toi pendant le déjeuner à l'école. Tu es fier/fière parce que tu t'es défendu(e) plusieurs fois!

 Brochure De temps en temps, tu aides ton père dans son agence de voyages. Il veut que tu l'aides à écrire un paragraphe sur la Guadeloupe pour sa nouvelle brochure. Ecris sept à huit lignes qui décrivent les jolies plages, les fonds marins et les créatures qu'on peut y trouver. Utilise aussi d'autres détails au sujet de la Guadeloupe que tu as appris dans ce chapitre.

 Conversation Ton cousin a toujours de bonnes blagues et toi, tu n'en as jamais. Pense à une blague qui va l'impressionner. Ensuite, écris une conversation entre ton cousin et toi où tu lui racontes ta blague et où il y réagit. Utilise entre sept et huit répliques pour la scène entière.

Copyright © by Holt, Rinehart and Winston. All rights reserved.

C D - R O M   A S S E S S M E N T

Laissez les bons temps rouler!

CD-ROM Assessment

Guided Recording

A toi de parler

Students record their responses to the following video prompts:

PROMPT 1 Qu'est-ce que tu penses de la musique de Louisiane? Qu'est-ce que tu préfères comme type de musique? Pourquoi?

PROMPT 2 Ça te branche de jouer des instruments de musique? Quel instrument est-ce que tu aimes le mieux?

PROMPT 3 Ça te plaît, la cuisine cajun? Qu'est-ce que tu aimes comme hors-d'œuvre?

PROMPT 4 Tu aimes le jambalaya? Qu'est-ce qu'on met dedans?

PROMPT 5 Comment tu trouves les fruits de mer ici? Qu'est-ce que tu préfères comme fruits de mer?

Guided Writing

A toi d'écrire

Students choose from among the following four writing scenarios. The first topic emphasizes the writing process.

 Histoire Tu écris un livre d'enfants sur les traditions cajuns. Prépare une conversation entre un petit garçon ou une petite fille et ses grands-parents qui habitent en Louisiane. L'enfant ne comprend pas bien les traditions cajuns, donc, il/elle pose beaucoup de questions et ses grands-parents lui répondent.

 Journal Imagine que tu reviens de Baton Rouge où tu es allé(e) à Mardi gras. Tu ne veux pas oublier cette expérience, alors tu la décris dans ton journal en sept ou huit lignes. Dis ce que tu as trouvé intéressant chez les gens, dans leurs costumes et dans la musique que tu as entendue.

 Interview Ton professeur a invité un Cajun à venir dans ta classe de français. Il/Elle veut que tu prépares sept ou huit questions basées sur ce que tu sais de la culture cajun. Au début de chaque question, donne ton impression sur l'aspect de la culture cajun dont tu parles.

 Lettre Il y a deux ans, tu as fait la connaissance d'une fille de Louisiane et maintenant, tu vas lui rendre visite. Avant ton voyage, tu veux savoir si ce que tu te rappelles de ton amie et de sa famille est vrai. Dans une lettre de sept ou huit lignes, demande à ton amie de confirmer tes souvenirs.

Have students follow these steps to complete their story.

PRELIMINAIRES Ecris quatre à cinq questions sur la nourriture, la musique de Louisiane et l'origine du mot "cajun".

REDACTION Ecris la scène en sept ou huit phrases. Dans cette scène, l'enfant pose les questions des PRELIMINAIRES et ses grands-parents y répondent.

RELECTURE Imprime ton histoire, relis-la et fais les changements nécessaires. N'oublie pas de vérifier l'orthographe, les accents et les majuscules.

CD-ROM ASSESS

Copyright © by Holt, Rinehart and Winston. All rights reserved.

Echanges sportifs et culturels

CD-ROM Assessment

Guided Recording

A toi de parler

Students imagine they are reporters covering the Olympics and they use the images they see and the following textual prompts to record commentaries.

PROMPT 1 Précise quel sport ces hommes pratiquent et imagine leurs nationalités. Donne tes prédictions sur qui va gagner l'épreuve et dis pourquoi.

PROMPT 2 Dis quel sport cette femme pratique. Imagine son nom et sa nationalité. Parle du matériel qu'elle utilise et dis si tu penses qu'elle va gagner l'épreuve.

PROMPT 3 Dis que tu es impatient(e) de voir cette épreuve. Imagine les nationalités du champion et du perdant et donne tes prédictions sur le résultat de l'épreuve.

PROMPT 4 Imagine la nationalité de ce champion et explique ce qu'il est en train de faire. Exprime ton admiration et dis qu'il va gagner.

Guided Writing

A toi d'écrire

Students choose from among the following four writing scenarios.

 Carte postale Tu vas assister à un tournoi d'athlétisme avec ta famille. C'est un long voyage et il te tarde d'arriver. Pendant le voyage, écris une carte postale à ton amie Julie où tu exprimes ton impatience en sept ou huit lignes. Dis-lui aussi ce que tu veux voir et faire pendant le tournoi.

 Journal Tu vas regarder les Jeux olympiques à la télé cet été. Ecris tes impressions dans ton journal. Pour certaines épreuves, tu penses savoir quels pays vont gagner; pour d'autres épreuves, tu as des doutes. Donne tes prédictions et exprime tes doutes en sept ou huit lignes.

 Catalogue Tu produis du matériel de sport à vendre à des magasins. Crée un catalogue où tu décris le matériel que tu produis pour différents sports. Donne aussi le prix de chaque article et laisse assez d'espace pour coller des illustrations. N'oublie pas de donner le nom de ta marque.

 Interview Tu dois faire un compte rendu sur un pays étranger pour ta classe de géographie. Pour t'aider, tu vas interviewer un athlète africain. Prépare huit ou neuf questions à lui poser au sujet de la vie quotidienne dans son pays.

Copyright © by Holt, Rinehart and Winston. All rights reserved.

CD-ROM ASSESSMENT